10 Lessons Learned From
Sheep & Shuttles

A.J. Delmonte & K.G. Ruehl

Sheep & Shuttles 🐑

Ten Lessons Learned From Sheep and Shuttles
Copyright © 2013 by A. J. Delmonte and K. G. Ruehl

Published by Your Answer Key.

Book and jacket design by Sandra L. Pagliughi
Jacket images: Shutterstock.com

ISBN-13: 978-0615849805
ISBN-10: 0615849806

For more information, visit www.youranswerkey.com;
or www.sheepandshuttles.com

To see Sheep and Shuttles photographs and more,
Like us at Facebook.com/sheepandshuttles

10 Lessons Learned From
Sheep & Shuttles

Sheep & Shuttles 🐑

Acknowledgements

From Keith

It is with deep love and appreciation that I want to thank the following individuals who have contributed directly or indirectly to the creation of this book. My lovely bride of 24 years Barbie, who continues to offer support and encouragement for my varied and at times unconventional projects. My handsome son Alex, whose inherent wit, creativity, and kind heart never fail to entertain us. My beautiful daughter Katarina, whose intellect, work ethic, and athletic ability continually amazes me. My father Gary, whose sound rational guidance throughout my life, which I've often ignored, is always appreciated. My step-father and co-author Tony, whose never wavering commitment to me and my family is cherished. My Grandma Staszak, whose corny sense of humor and energetic lifestyle contradicts her 90 year old 4'11" frame and is a true inspiration well beyond her 21 grandchildren and 16 great-grandchildren. My sister-in-law Sandy, whose assistance with the artistry and layout of the book was top-notch. My 30 year-long friend Greg, whose solution orientated positive attitude has been invaluable to me. Greg's wife Melissa, for her excellent editing assistance. Friends Barry and Mike, whose active participation in several of the stories told in this book will always be remembered. Countless other family and friends who have provided support over the years.

Sheep & Shuttles

Acknowledgements

From Tony

By the time you reach my stage in life, there are so many people to thank for helping you to get to that stage that it's impossible to remember them all. But if I concentrate on those that have had the most influence in this project, it helps to narrow it down. First and foremost of course is my family. My stepson and co-author, Keith, of course who has continually said that his goal in life was to make my semi-retirement as busy as possible was the major catalyst. He has been as close to me as my own son since he was four years old. My wonderful son, Tony, whose intellectual political views continually cause me to reevaluate my own views, has also been a constant source of pride. Next is my beautiful daughter, Patti, who continuously amazes me with her persistence and determination to improve the education system in this country. She has always held a special place in my heart. By far, the greatest debt of gratitude goes to my wonderful and loving wife, Trudy. She has changed my life in more ways than I can describe, and has supported me in every wild hair I have attempted. She truly is the light of my life, who never hesitates to tell me when my head is getting too big for my shoulders.

I would be remiss if I didn't mention the hundreds of super-intelligent people that I had the pleasure of working with at Kennedy Space Center. While some of them refer to me as their mentor, I have learned far more from them than they could have ever learned from me.

Sheep & Shuttles

Forward

A Word From Keith

Our family's passion for animals has allowed us to play host to an ever changing menagerie. A visit to the Ruehl household, for the past 8 years near Asheville, North Carolina and for the 8 years prior to that in Jupiter, Florida, would have found some combination of the following: a pack of dogs, cats, chickens, geese, ducks, peacocks, turkeys, horses, potbelly pigs, goats, sheep, mice, rabbits, a donkey, emus, a llama, bees, a turtle, a rat, and alligators (uninvited).

A few basic rules have governed our collection of creatures. First, no animals reside in the house. Dictated by cleanliness and common sense, this rule has only been broken with rodents and reptiles that are relegated to their respective self-contained homes within our home. Second, all family members participate in the animal care. Despite forever being outnumbered, my wife Barbie, son Alex, daughter Katarina, and I manage with varying degrees of success to house, feed, groom, and doctor them all. Third, generally speaking we don't eat our pets.

A Word From Tony

As Keith's step-father since he was about four years old, I always knew of his love for animals. I must say, however, that I was more than just a little surprised when that love turned into a full-blown menagerie after marrying his beautiful wife Barbie. Visits to his home over the years always included stories of the latest adventure along with the latest additions to the zoo. I, among others, began to encourage Keith to put pen to paper and pass these stories on for others to enjoy.

In early 2012 the conversations became serious, and after some discussion we decided to make it a collaborative effort. I had spent my working career leading large and small organizations, eighteen years of which were spent working in the Space Shuttle program at Kennedy Space Center. As we discussed the animal stories, it became clear that there was a business or leadership lesson that could be learned from each one of them. The result is ten life and leadership lessons. We hope you enjoy them.

Chapter 1

"Sheep" ishness

"I want to get some sheep." Not a typical response when you ask your spouse what she would like for Christmas. However, I must admit, I was not terribly shocked when this was the reply my wife Barbara gave after I asked the routine seasonal question.

We had recently moved to the mountains of North Carolina from Florida. Upon further discussion with Barbara I learned that for years she had suppressed the shepherding desire due to the fact she believed that it would be cruel and inhumane to own wool coat wearing critters in south Florida.

It was our "third rule," we don't eat our pets , that gave me immediate pause regarding Barbara's request for sheep. "What are we going to do with the sheep if we get them?" I asked my wife while trying to remember what aisle the mint jelly was on at our local supermarket. Quickly reminding me of our "no eat pet policy" she explained that we could make money off them by selling their wool.

Barbara is a third grade teacher, which I truly believe it is her calling. She possesses certain inherent qualities that make her exceptional at what she does. Her passion, unconditional commitment, and deep caring for her students are highly evident. These same qualities serve us well when it comes to caring for our critters (kids and animals). I am a business major. I owned a company for about ten years and currently work within a business environment. My strengths should include an ability to objectively analyze an issue and determine sufficient return on investment.

Given these different sets of strengths, there was no doubt whose responsibility it was to determine if sheep ownership was economically feasible for our family. "So, how much are sheep anyway?" I asked my wife.

"$50 to $100 dollars" she nonchalantly replied.

"How many are we going to get?" I inquired realizing that I was quickly being suckered in by a superior wit.

"Only 4 or 5" she replied with a shoulder shrug as if to imply no big deal.

"What do they eat?" I asked noticing an almost instant eye roll and sigh from my bride as she sarcastically replied "Grass...Duuuuh."

Chapter 1

"Where will they live?" seemed to be the next logical question.

Barbara, struggling to be patient with my tiresome questions replied "We will put up some fencing and a simple lean-to."

Now I'm not sure whether it was temporary insanity or simply the realization that if I chose to debate the issue I would ultimately find myself building a dog house rather than a "simple lean-to" but the next phrase I uttered "OK, let's get some" would change our lives for years to come.

Over the course of the next two months I was educated on proper pasture and shelter accommodations as we prepared for the eventual arrival of our flock of ruminates. As it turned out we needed to fence in two separate sections of our property so we could alternate pastures allowing for one to recover while the cuddly creatures gently grazed on the other. After some deliberation, considering the cost and installation time and effort, we decided to erect a cattle panel and t-post fence. Don't feel bad, I had no idea what a "cattle panel" was either. This would be the first of a long list of terms that I would be adding to my regular vocabulary.

It only took two thousand dollars and two weekends of driving t-posts and hanging cattle panels to create our two pastures. A couple observations about putting up fencing in the mountains… Mountains by definition have a lot of rocks which are the enemy of digging or driving. This was especially enlightening to this Florida boy who was used to digging a three foot hole in the sand with a plastic spoon. Second, making the end product look good is much easier on flat land… which we have none of. Additionally, here is an important safety note that I learned the hard way… t-post drivers (picture a steel cylinder about the size of two Pringles containers end-to-end with two handles and heavily weighted on the closed end and used in lieu of a sledge hammer to pound metal t-posts into the ground) may cause concussions if not used properly.

The next order of business was to build a shelter for each of the pastures. We decided on a basic lean-to with a metal roof. I learned that there was no discount offered for the lumber, fasteners, and metal roof panels based on the fact that they were going to be used to erect a simple structure to hold farm animals. Twelve hundred dollars and two weekends later we had our sheep shelters.

"Ok Honey… we're ready for the sheep…" I somewhat proudly announced to my wife.

"Almost" she matter-of-factly replied. "We need a guard animal" she quickly added.

"A guard animal?" I skeptically inquired.

Chapter 1

"Yes, a guard animal to protect the sheep from coyotes."

"How about Fergus?" referring to our newly acquired Old English Sheep Dog.

She went on to explain that most dogs, including Sheep dogs, don't mix well with sheep but there are several different animals that may do the job including donkeys, llamas, and Great Pyrenees dogs.

"But why do they call them SHEEP DOGS" I persisted realizing we were on the edge of adding yet another animal to our menagerie.

After some additional guard animal research we landed on a two hundred dollar donkey to protect our flock... which is a story in itself that we will discuss later.

Barbie was already beginning to build her network of sheep subculture contacts and had identified four lambs to her liking that would serve as her Mother's Day gift. Cherokee and Chipawa were Cotswold ewes (female sheep) purchased for $75 each. Teton, and Tahoe where Cotswold/Border Lester mix whethers (castrated male sheep) costing $50 each. We easily loaded them up into the back of our SUV and headed towards home.

"Oh, we need to pick up some feed on the way" Barbie shouted over the continual BAAAAAAing (translated... Where's mommy, where's mommy, where's mommy,....) coming from the obviously very agitated lambs in the back of the truck.

"Feed?? I thought they ate grass?" I naively replied.

Well, as it turns out, you are supposed to supplement their grazing with a corn and protein mix. I liken this "supplement" to be crack for sheep in the respect that they will do anything to get their daily fix including running each other and you over.

Several months of religiously tending to the new flock passed and my wife announced it was time to get our sheep sheared. By this time their crack habit was up to 50 pounds per week and they had more than tripled in size.

Given neither of us had sheep shearing experience, Barbie arranged for a professional shearer to come to the house to give our cuddly critters their first haircut. The fee was $15 per sheep which didn't sound unreasonable to me since that's about what I would pay for my own haircut and I suspected sheep would be a tad more labor intensive because I typically would not kick, scream, and defecate while I was getting a trim.

I must admit, I was excited when shearing day arrived. This was going to be the big payoff for all of the time and money invested in this sheep venture. In case you weren't keeping track, below summarizes just some of the expenses not including our sweat equity:

Fencing materials	$2,000
Lean-to materials	$1,200
Donkey	$200
Sheep	$250
Feed (3 months)	$400
Worming meds	$120
Shearing	$60
Total	$4,230

Anthony, the shearer, was a chatty but efficient fellow. He obviously knew his sheep and was kind enough to attempt to teach me how to Judo the sheep into a submission position so one could shave them down to their skin without completely stressing out the sheep or yourself. With a combination of precision and speed Anthony sheared and simultaneously educated me on the finer points of sheep shearing with the intent of me performing this task in the future.

"You guys have done a really good job with these sheep. They look very healthy and the wool is top notch." Anthony complimented.

As Anthony finished up the last sheep I collected the detached wool with pride and expectancy of

the monetary payoff for all of our efforts. It filled
the large plastic garbage bag which I was effortlessly holding in one hand.

"So Anthony, how much can we get for this
wool?" I asked with a level of anticipation akin to
Christmas morning.

"Well, this is high quality wool." He replied
with a thoughtful dramatic pause. "I bet you could
fetch $4 to $5 per pound."

As I lifted the garbage bag up and down with
ease in my left hand I estimated that I was holding
about 7 pounds of wool... $35 worth!

Performing a quick and crude break-even
analysis in my head I came to the conclusion that
it would take over one hundred years to recoup
our initial investment and this calculation did not
include any ongoing operational expenses.

As I stood there literally and figuratively holding the bag I realized my failure... I had been
sheepish about business planning!!

The Lesson – Don't be sheepish about planning

On February 17, 1894 the New York Times ran
an article about the antics of financier C. L. Riker.
The article related a story, verified by many of his
friends, of an apple orchard venture that Riker
entered into with several of his relatives. Unhappy

with the conventional means for collecting the
fruit, however, which he deemed as expensive and
laborious, he sought other methods. He hit upon
an idea to introduce a number of monkeys into the
orchard, which he was convinced would pick the
fruit and drop it gently to the ground where it
could be easily gathered by workers.
Unfortunately, the monkeys saw the fruit as more
of a source of amusement, and pelted each other
with the few pieces of fruit that they picked. It
didn't take long for Riker to see the flaw in his
plan.

We all have probably, at some time in our lives,
charged into a venture that we were convinced was
the idea of a lifetime, only to find out that we had-
n't thought things through very well. Sometimes
they turn out well, sometimes they don't.
Sometimes they involve animals, sometimes they
don't. Riker's involved monkeys, Keith's and
Barbie's involved sheep!

Planning should be a precursor to embarking on
any venture. But what is planning anyway?
Planning is identifying where you are now, where
you want to go, and have at least a clue about how
you are going to get there. Planning is necessary
in order to provide a sense of direction and purpose.

As Keith and Barbie discovered, planning for

sheep farming requires more than just a passion for making it successful, and most ventures that are worth pursuing are no different. Since the title of this book is "Sheep and Shuttles", it's only appropriate that this first lesson comes from the U. S. Space Shuttle Program, where effective planning was always a constant for success.

Every space mission starts with an objective. That objective may be technical, scientific or political. Or, it may be a combination of all three. These objectives drive the planning process for the entire mission. This planning process may start several years before the actual launch, and includes a number of different aspects. One aspect focuses on the crew; the Astronauts who will fly on the mission. This phase of planning results in an excruciatingly detailed schedule of crew activities, giving a minute by minute timeline of everything that must take place from launch to landing. A typical timeline will include activities like: 40 minutes for "pre-sleep", which includes eating dinner, relaxing and taking care of personal hygiene before bedtime; 8 hours of sleep; and 45 minutes of "post-sleep", including waking up, doing personal hygiene, housekeeping and getting ready for the day's work.

Another aspect of the lengthy planning process is operations support planning. This phase of planning includes a description and schedule of all activities that need to be performed in order to ready the facilities, the vehicle, the various payloads and the controller personnel who will support the mission. Once again, this is done in mind-boggling detail, with a focus on safety and mission performance.

A third aspect of the planning is the flight design and dynamics plan. This is where the detailed flight profile is developed, including the requirements for vehicle ascent trajectory; navigation and guidance; orbit shaping; separation and collision avoidance; payload deployment; rendezvous operations; proximity operations; and descent and landing operations.

Most projects, organizations or activities don't come close to requiring the level of planning that came to be routine in the Space Shuttle program. But on the other hand, most projects, organizations and activities are not facing the same level of risk. Being sheepish about planning for making profit selling wool is quite different from being able to successfully launch seven people into orbit, have them perform mind-numbing feats while there, and return them safely to earth. But it's still necessary for success.

The planning process in the space shuttle program did not happen by accident. Likewise, in any venture worth pursuing, planning needs to be well-thought-out, deliberate and painstaking. Effective business planning aids in making the most effective use of financial and human resources, and is key to meeting the objectives of the venture.

Chapter 2

Birds & Bird Dogs

We had just moved from a home in the suburbs with a yard slightly larger than the footprint of the house, which significantly restricted our ability to act on our love of animals, to a more rural setting in Jupiter, FL. The new homestead was complete with a reasonably sized house, pond, and barn all located on six acres. Needless to say we were excited and anxious to create a mini-farm environment for our young family.

A couple of trips to the animal shelter and an inability to agree on which dog to bring home netted our first three additions; a white lab which my five year old son inexplicably named Hospin, a chocolate lab we not so creatively named Hershey, and a white-pawed black spaniel mix we named Sox. All three seemed to get along well with each other and everyone in the family.

Shortly after obtaining the pack of dogs, we set our sights on fowl. I built a dog house style coop on stilts, with the surrounding area fenced in with chicken wire and then added about a dozen poults (baby turkeys). Simultaneously we began raising a clutch of chicks, and ducklings, in one of the barn stalls. We thought the ducks would be a cool addition to the pond, the chickens would provide eggs, and the turkeys would provide ambiance.

We had discussed the potential threats to our new fowl which included raccoons, opossum, hawks, panthers, and alligators to name a few. We had taken reasonable precautions for novice caretakers using copious quantities of chicken wire and diligently cooping-up our fledgling flocks nightly. For weeks, multiple times per day, we tended to our chirping nurseries ensuring that all had proper amounts of water, food, warmth, shelter, and protection.

The young turkeys were growing at an impressive rate and had me silently questioning the practicality of our "no eat pet" policy. I had visions of wide-eyed lip-licking extended family circled around the Thanksgiving Day feast with dual glistening crispy skinned home grown birds as centerpieces. Yes sir, this year would be especially meaningful as we toasted with gratitude not only to health and prosperity but also to the pilgrims with whom we now share the pride of self-sufficiency!

Chapter 2

In the dim light of the early morning ritual I made the short trek to the turkey coop to tend to the poults basic needs and contemplate which two would be lucky enough to eventually grace our dining room table. In bewilderment I came to an abrupt stop when I spotted Sox inside of the heavily fortified coop. There was now a fresh pile of excavated dirt just outside the chicken wire and Sox was inside laying on his belly gnawing on some unidentifiable object grasped between his snowy front paws. As I drew closer he continued his task at hand with complete indifference to my presence. I began to take in the horrific scene of mutilated baby turkeys scattered throughout the coop in varying degrees of completeness. Sox had killed them all and was now intently gorging himself on the spoils of his hunt. Anger, sadness, and guilt flooded over me as I glared at Sox who nonchalantly looked up at me as if to say "Would you like to join me... here have a leg?" Too disgusted and angry to think clearly, I interrupted Sox's breakfast buffet by yelling some unintelligible expletives while grabbing his collar and not so gently escorting him out of the coop.

After burying the victims of the slaughter in a mass grave I made the executive decision that a cold hearted killer would not live amongst us and Sox would have to go. Fearing that a firing squad may attract unwanted attention I opted for an undetermined jail sentence by taking him back to the animal shelter. When asked why I was returning this fine animal I simply cited irreconcilable differences and told the keeper that when Sox made it out on parole there should be a restraining order prohibiting any close interaction with fowl.

Life on the fledgling farm returned to its typical less violent state as we continued to raise the young flock of chickens and ducks. The chicks were relocated to the refortified coop and the ducks had a barn stall all to themselves. The chicks were fully feathered and allowed to venture outside the coop under our watchful protection. Similarly, the ducks had outgrown their oversized water bowl and were now periodically let out to make the short waddle over to the pond. Hershey and Hospin for the most part seemed to disregard the fowl except when their feathered friends would attempt to muscle in to their dog bowls at feeding time. These ill-advised raids would inevitably end with one of the dogs lunging at the food thieves, a few intense warning barks, an outburst of terrified clucks or quacks, and a small cloud of detached feathers drifting back to the ground. I did little to intervene, naively figuring that the fowl would get the message and learn to stay away from the hungry hounds.

Chapter 2

We became more relaxed about letting the chickens and ducks free range. The remaining two dogs showed little interest in dining on the birds and they were effective at keeping most of the predators away. All seemed to be in harmony, the hens were dutifully laying eggs and the ducks were gracefully swimming in the pond. Then we found a dead duck in the yard. It was a female Rohen that we had named Daisy (not to be confused with a subsequent canine acquisition). There were signs of a struggle but Daisy was in surprisingly good shape... other than being dead of course. We speculated that a predator must have entered the yard, killed Daisy, and then been scared off by one of our ever attentive canines.

Over the next couple of weeks, one-by-one, we found similar gruesome crime scenes. While discussing our unwanted attrition with a knowledgeable neighbor, he pointed out that it was very unusual that a predator would leave behind its prey and it was much more likely that our labs were the culprits. He articulated what we didn't want to admit; that most likely we were to blame. We had forced birds and bird dogs into the same confined habitat and expected them to coexist peacefully.

Somewhat in denial we solicited advice on how to remedy the conflict. Numerous methods were suggested. Most of them would have made the Dog Whisperer shout "NO!" But in desperation, following each carcass discovery we tried them one-by-one including confinement, a smack with a newspaper, yelling, and my personal favorite of tying the dead fowl to the dog's collar and letting it ripen for two days. Shockingly, none of these techniques proved to be effective. The killings continued until the flock was all but gone.

During this time frame Hershey and Hospin also began a daily routine of escaping from our fenced yard and gallivanting around the neighborhood. They would inevitably return in the evening before feeding time. Despite our best efforts we were unable to determine how they made their great escape let alone prevent them from repeating it the next day. Our frustration with the bird murdering Houdini hounds reached a climax when they returned one evening and we noticed a note carefully wrapped and attached to Hospin's collar. The note read "Please keep your dogs in your yard. They just dug up my dead cat."

The next day the dogs absconded as usual but never returned. After a couple of phone calls we determined that they had been picked up by animal control. We rushed out, bypassing the pound, and purchased a new flock of fowl, our way of managing conflict.

Chapter 2

The Lesson – Manage Conflict

Conflict in organizations is as predictable as bringing birds and bird dogs together. Particularly in the high-tech environment we live and work in today, where teams are almost always made up of diverse skills, backgrounds and personalities. Sometimes, as with Hershey and Hospin, some of the offenders leave, and the problems take care of themselves. More often than not, though, all of the team members are important contributors in their own way, and because most team members don't choose their own counterparts, the conflict must be dealt with. And that's usually the job of management.

From a management standpoint it's important to be able to distinguish between healthy and unhealthy conflict. Management consultant, Patrick Lencioni, defines healthy conflict as accountability to other team members. Accountability on a team means being vulnerable, or open to being challenged by team members when necessary, such as when a team member is not following through on commitments, or not performing up to par. Lencioni's work deals primarily with executive management teams, but the concept applies to teams at all levels. Unless team members, and hence the team as a whole, can readily accept constructive inquiry into the values and assumptions in use, they will never become a fully functioning team. Conflict of this sort results in strengthening of the team and improved overall effectiveness.

Unhealthy conflict on the other hand is a completely different thing and requires quick and decisive intervention by management. This type of conflict results in a destruction of morale and creates a divisive, rather than cohesive environment. Left unchecked, unhealthy conflict will quickly sap the energy of a team and lead to a hostile work environment. As a manager, knowing when to intervene is important and requires some knowledge about team dynamics. In 1965, Dr. Bruce W. Tuckman published a short article that put forth a now widely used model of team development that can provide some clues.

According to Tuckman's model, every team goes through four stages of development. He dubbed the four stages forming, storming, norming and performing. Forming is the first stage, when the group members' main concern is orienting themselves to identify the boundaries from a task and interpersonal behavior standpoint. The storming stage follows forming and is where healthy conflict can be mistaken for unhealthy. During this stage there is a lot of jockeying for position in an attempt to define each member's role with respect to the group. It's extremely important for the team and the respective management to recognize that this is an important part of the team's development. Intervention too early can be detrimental to the team's ability to learn to resolve its own healthy conflict.

In the norming stage, team cohesiveness begins to develop, standards and roles are adopted and the healthy practice of inquiry is accepted by members. Finally in the performing stage, the team begins to think, act and function as a well-oiled machine, and task performance becomes the primary objective. The key thing to understand about the Tuckmann model is that virtually all teams will go through these stages which are necessary to the healthy transition from group to team.

In another article by Thomas Cappozzoli, some additional guidelines are provided to help recognize healthy versus unhealthy conflict. According to Cappozzoli's research, indicators of healthy conflict include:

- People change and grow from the conflict
- It results in a solution to the problem
- It increases involvement of those affected
- It builds cohesiveness among the team members

On the other hand, indicators of unhealthy conflict include:
- No decision is reached and problems are unsolved
- Energy is diverted to non-value activities
- Morale deteriorates
- The team becomes divided and polarized

The use of teams in organizational settings is here for the long term and the value to be derived from effective, functioning teams cannot be understated. Waiting for the bird dogs to leave on their own, when the birds are your priority is not an effective management approach. So knowing when to intervene and when to leave the team alone can be the difference between success and failure.

The Intimidator

Our hobby farm in southeast Florida was beginning to take shape. We were able to rent out a couple of stalls in the barn as a partial boarding arrangement. Which means that the horse owners paid us to use our barn and surrounding pasture and they did all of the feeding and caring of the horses themselves. In addition to the obvious financial benefit of this agreement we gained much enjoyment from the mere presence of the horses which lent a degree of legitimacy to our little farm. At this time, additional residents included a flock of chickens, several bird friendly dogs, two identical looking black barn cats, a pair of geese that were more protective of the property than the dogs, a caged rabbit, and a wild peacock that flew in one afternoon, and once fed, decided to stick around. All of these critters cohabitated with little conflict and seemed to respect, or at the very least, tolerate each other.

While performing the daily chores one morning I happened to glance over the one acre pond situated on our property directly behind the house. The early dawn light and the wispy fog hanging just above the water's surface gave the scene an eerie appearance. I caught a glimpse of a log-like object floating near the middle of the pond. As I approached the water's edge to take a closer look I realized that the "log" was glaring back at me. In fact, it was an alligator. As I stood there staring at this prehistoric looking creature my first thought was "Cool... we have a new pet." Then I began to consider how he may interact with the other animals... or worse yet with our young kids. Visions of alligator death rolls, explosions of feathers, and screaming kids flooded my thoughts. With no thought of the ridiculousness of my action I promptly heaved a sizable rock in the general direction of the trespasser and shouted "GO HOME!" The gator gazed at me with a smile as if to say "I am home" and slowly disappeared below the surface.

Although alligators were once almost hunted to extinction, under governmental protection the populations have rebounded significantly over the past few decades. Spotting gators sunning themselves on golf courses and in canals alongside roads had become common-place in South Florida. They remain protected, not so much because of a concern for their numbers, but because of their similar appearance to the American Crocodile which is truly endangered. Generally, if left alone, alligators were harmless. However, there is nothing like one showing up in your backyard to raise your level of concern. Even though our intruder was only about four feet long there was little doubt in my mind that if he was so inclined he could devour some of our smaller pets and could significantly injure our larger inhabitants, kids included.

Since alligators are protected it is unlawful to harass, capture, or kill them even if they are on your property. With that in mind, I called the alligator removal hotline figuring a trapper would be quickly sent out to relocate our unwanted visitor. "Where is the alligator?" asked the voice with a bored matter-of-fact tone. "In a pond in my backyard" I replied sensing the lack of concern over my situation. "How big is the alligator?" the voice continued. "About 4 feet" I answered. "OK… we'll put you on the list." Her rehearsed non-committal responses to my questions regarding when I should expect to see the trapper, and what was going to happen to the unfortunate crocodilian once removed would have made a campaigning politician proud.

Over the next several days we altered our routine to accommodate the presence of the interloper. We gave the kids strict instructions to avoid playing with, or near, the gator and watched over them whenever they were outside. We also kept an eye on all of the other critters especially when they ventured down to the pond to quench their thirst. Weeks went by without incident and our resident reptilian seemed content to spend his days sunning himself on the shore of the pond and taking an occasional dip. He showed no interest in any of the other inhabitants and was now referred to in the household as "Ally". Our paranoia over his presence soon vanished…and then so did he. Without so much as a thank you he up and left. I must admit I was a bit saddened by Ally's sudden departure. I'm not sure whether my feelings were due to the loss of one of our beloved tenants or the loss of a conversation starter with guests…. "Hey come see our pet alligator…"

A month after his leaving, which was approximately two months after his arrival and my call to the hotline, we received a call from the state trapper saying he was ready to come out and remove the alligator from our premises. I kindly thanked him for his call and informed him that the gator in question had moved on.

A couple of months after our first guest gator left, our second arrived. Apparently word had spread within the alligator community that if you were looking for a peaceful place to chill for a few weeks the Ruehl house was ideal. It took only minutes to realize that unlike our first boarder our latest guest was an extrovert. When we or any of the animals approached the edge of the pond he would immediately come over to investigate. Although he was about the same size as Ally his demeanor was polar opposite of his docile predecessor. With a sense of urgency I called the alligator removal hotline again and had virtually the identical conversation as previously.

Our alligator paranoia now renewed we kept vigilant watch over the pond. Two days after Ally2's arrival I heard a shriek from the kitchen. I ran in to see my wife Barbie pointing through the kitchen window towards the pond and screaming "The alligator is going to eat Elvis!!" For clarification, she was not referring to the legendary singer, but rather to our Black Polish Rooster which we had named Elvis due the striking resemblance of his jet black feathered hairdo and his crooning capabilities to that of the late great entertainer. Staring through the window I saw Elvis casually swimming across the pond with the gator quickly closing the approximate 20 foot gap between the two. I immediately ran out of the house and straight into the pond only slowing down briefly to snag a couple of rocks from the shoreline. When the water was waste high I had a fleeting flash of sanity that caused me to pause, rather than proceeding to swim out towards the oblivious chicken and the menacing predator in deeper water 10 yards from where I was standing. The gator was only a couple feet behind Elvis and still gaining when I shouted and threw a rock towards the pair. It landed between the rooster's tail and the gator's snout. Seemingly startled, the alligator quickly submerged below the surface, and apparently unaware of his narrowly averted doom, the ignorant rooster continued his carefree swim towards the shore where I snatched him up and delivered him safely to the coop.

After the adrenaline wore off I began to contemplate the oddity of the episode. We had never seen a chicken in the pond before. I had assumed that they didn't swim because there were only two instances that I had seen our chickens in water. The first was in a pot on the stove when we broke our "no eat pet" policy to deal with a couple of particularly aggressive roosters. The second was when I fished a dead one (which had apparently drowned due to pure stupidity) out of a horse's water bucket. So seeing Elvis swimming duck like across the pond was a first; not to mention him being pursued by a hungry gator. Upon reflection I suppose that some may view my behavior in this situation as odd also. If it had been captured on video, the newscast teaser that evening may have been "News at eleven… lunatic runs into pond to save a swimming chicken…"

Determined to not let the pond squatter impact our outdoor enjoyment, the kids and I donned life preservers and piled into the canoe for a boat ride around the pond which I had promised them would be on the agenda for the weekend. I brought along a miniature remote controlled plastic speed boat, which we planned to take turns driving from the canoe. Being the largest kid on the boat I got to go first. As I maneuvered the toy boat in circles around our canoe I spotted the gator on the surface of the water about fifteen yards away. I decided to try to spook him before he had a chance to come over to investigate the humans in his domain. I made a wide circle with the speed boat allowing it to get up to full speed and guided it directly towards the alligator. Fully anticipating the gator to submerge as the mini boat approached I kept the throttle firmly pressed down with my thumb. To my astonishment and the kids' wide-eyed delight the gator didn't submerge and the speed boat launched out of the water as it hit him in the head right behind his eyes. Feeling somewhat guilty I instructed the kids to not run over our gator as they took their turns with the speed boat.

Over the course of the next few days the alligator's aggressive behavior escalated. I'm not sure whether it was attributed to his growing hunger or just being vindictive about being hit in the head with a speed boat. He would approach the horses ever closer every time they stood in the water, and our boarder expressed a concern about the potential for the gator to harm the lower legs of the horses. The final straw was when the gator clamped down on the front leg of one of our dogs, a small terrier mix named Riggs, while he was lapping up a midday refreshment at the water's edge. Riggs let out a human-like blood curdling yelp and was able to escape from the jaws of certain death. All of the residents on our tiny farm were on edge due to our threatening unwanted guest gator and it seemed just a matter of time before tragedy would strike.

Having not heard any response from my most recent call to the alligator hotline, I decided it was time to take action to return relative peace and safety to our extended household. Since Barbie had no interest in cooking gator fritters and our guest was too small to make a proper sized pair of boots for myself, I decided to relocate the misplaced crocodilian. After several failed attempts to catch him with a hook and line, I was growing anxious and increasingly more concerned for the welfare of our family. Out of desperation driven by protective instinct, I waded out into the water up to my knees and waited for the intimidating habitant to arrive. Less than two minutes later he was fearlessly a few short feet from where I was standing and looked as though he was contemplating which of my legs he was going to latch onto with his powerful jaws. I held my breath and peppered him with a blast of buck-shot which had the desired effect of stunning him long enough for me to grab him and throw him in the back of my truck. I transported him to a canal a few miles away, where we said our goodbyes as he slid into the water and swam off. The Intimidator was gone and peace again reigned on the homestead.

The Lesson – Eliminate Intimidation

Few of us are required to battle alligators in our day to day business dealings. But it's hard to deny that we, as leaders, must do everything in our power to protect those who depend on us in times of peril. Again, the lesson comes from America's space program.

The Apollo Space program began in the 1960s, and after John F. Kennedy's challenge to put a man on the moon, became a source of pride to all

Americans. It also became the source of thousands of well-paying jobs and tremendous growth in the Central Florida area and in particular Brevard County. Prior to 1960 the county was home to approximately 24,000 people. By the mid-1960s that number grew to almost 115,000. The positive impact was felt across the board, not just in the technical industries needed to support the space program, but also in banking, insurance, construction and real estate.

In spite of a few hiccups due to politically related funding issues, the area continued to prosper as the moon missions took place and then were replaced by Skylab and eventually the Space Shuttle in 1972. The Space Coast was also becoming one of the top tourist attractions in the State of Florida with the opening of the Kennedy Space Center visitor's center. With the advent of the Disney theme parks in the early 70s, Disney tourists also spilled over to the Space Coast, enhancing the area even further. By the mid-70s thousands of family livelihoods, in all walks of life, depended on the U.S. space program.

Then, in 1986, disaster struck. On January 28th, seventy-three seconds into its launch, the Space Shuttle Challenger exploded, disintegrating over the Atlantic Ocean and killing its seven crew members. In the wake of the disaster, all future

Shuttle flights were grounded. The accident was devastating to the Shuttle workers in many ways, but probably the greatest impact was the number of employees that were sent to the unemployment lines. Personnel cutbacks in the 1970s, as programs transitioned from one to the other, had also resulted in the loss of critically-skilled employees, and because of the overall dependence on the space business, extreme hardship for the entire area.

The post-Challenger cutback proved to be no different, with the flight hiatus lasting close to three years. Even though the Space Coast businesses were more diversified now, the impact was still painful. While the ensuing investigation continued there was no work for many of the critically-skilled engineers and technicians, so needing to feed their families, many left the area and never returned.

Shuttle flights resumed on September 29th, 1988, with the successful launch of Discovery on a four day mission. The loss of critical skills that occurred after Challenger was expensive and painful to recover from, but eventually the team was rebuilt and the area once again began to prosper. Successful Shuttle flights continued for fifteen years. Many improvements were made in flight hardware and processes and the team became stronger than ever. Then, disaster struck again.

On February 1st, 2003 The Space Shuttle Columbia broke up on reentry, due to wing damage that had occurred during launch and went undetected. Again, seven crew members were killed and Shuttle flights were curtailed. This time, however, it appeared that some lessons had been learned from past experience. The first priority, of course, was recovery of the vehicle and the remains of the crew. The second priority was investigating the causes, but very high on the priority list was taking care of the people who depended on the program for their livelihood, and preserving critical skills for return to flight. Commitments were made by NASA and the Shuttle contractors, that they would not again place themselves at risk of losing those critical-skills.

The flight hiatus this time was over two years, with Discovery once again being the return to flight vehicle on July 26th, 2005. During that period, not a single person was furloughed, with the time being used for strengthening the team through training, and making improvements to the facilities, hardware and processes. The experience spoke volumes about the leadership and courage of the decision-makers to protect the people that depended on them. Rather than being intimidated

Chapter 3

by an alligator in the form of the threat of unemployment, a protracted job search and potential relocation of their families, the team was able to ignore the lurking alligator and focus on what was necessary for a smooth return to flight.

Sheep & Shuttles 🐑

Chapter 4

Pushing Up Daisy

"Whatever you do… DO NOT BRING HOME THE BASSEST HOUND!" The inflection in Barbara's voice left no doubt that this was not merely a recommendation but rather a demand with threatening undertones. She issued this edict as we were passing in our driveway. She had visited the local animal shelter on her way home from work and as she was arriving home I was just leaving to head to the shelter. She went on to briefly describe a black harry terrier mix that she had seen and felt would make a good addition to our hobby farm.

As I perused the ample selection of homeless hounds, I spotted the ungroomed dreadlock sporting terrier that my sympathetic bride had her eye on. My view of this mutt was far less compassionate, and I may have blurted out a bit too loudly that if you added a handle you would have yourself a pretty good mop.

A few cages down however, was the Basset
Hound that I had been cautioned about. As I stared
at this living proof that God has a sense of humor
I couldn't help but laugh aloud at the site of her.
She looked as though she had been created with
random leftover parts from various more purpose-
fully contrived canines. I now realized that the distinct hound howling I heard in the background
since my arrival was coming from this sad eyed,
grey bearded creature. Her sorrowful constant
crooning reminded me of a condemned prisoner
singing the blues, having given up on any potential stay of execution and resolved to the fact that
his final walk was looming. I knew it was my duty
to save this wretched soul and give her a second
chance at life. Without hesitation and with no
thought of the potential consequences of my
humanitarian effort, I quickly completed the necessary paperwork and loaded her into my truck.

Daisy sat in the passenger seat occasionally
glancing over at me as if to say "Thank you kind
fellow… I will be forever grateful to you for sav-
ing my life." As we got closer to home I recalled
the ominous warning Barbie had issued a couple
of short hours prior. Surely Barbie would have a
change of heart once she realized we rescued this
doomed doggie.

As we pulled into the driveway Barbie came

out to greet us. When Daisy, with significant effort and assistance, made it out of the truck and came into Barbie's view, I immediately realized that Daisy may have company in the dog house that night. Unfortunately, Barbie was not swayed by my altruistic argument and she made it very clear that my inconsiderate rebuff of her request was not appreciated. To reaffirm her discontent with an added degree of emotional reimbursement, she defiantly delivered the Rastafarian terrier, promptly named Chewie, to our doorstep the next day.

Over the next week Daisy and Chewie settled in and Barbie settled down. My buddy Greg and I decided to blow off some steam on the weekend by hitting a few golf balls in the backyard. Up to that point my golf experience had consisted of serious play on various courses with functional wee windmills and colorfully painted prehistoric predators, and a couple of inebriated outings on a "real" course. As Daisy lazily lounged in the assuredly safe zone of the four o'clock position and fifteen yards from our centrally located tee, Greg hit a respectable twelve o'clock straight 150 yard shot over our pond. Determined to top his shot, with brute strength I crushed the ball. It came off my driver with impressive velocity, and nearly impossible trajectory of a heat seeking missile, finding its target square between Daisy's eyes. Her entire body lifted two feet off the ground as if her short stubby legs were spring loaded, and then she came crashing back to earth landing in a motionless heap. Convinced I would be spending the rest of the evening burying our new arrival, we ran to her side and found her drifting back into consciousness. With her eyes still unfocused and a trickle of blood beginning to show at her nostrils, swelling at the point of impact began. Before long she had a knot the size of.... well... a golf ball just above her brow line.

Feeling more than a tad guilty I spent a mostly sleepless night close by Daisy's side, periodically feeding her medication laced cheese balls. On the occasions I did drift off to sleep my dreams were filled with a Sumo sized animal control officer bent on whipping my ass with a nine iron. Fortunately Daisy survived. And aside from a propensity to chew my golf shoes into unrecognizable leather masses and permanently hide several sleeves of golf balls, she seemed quite normal and my nine iron nightmares slowly waned.

Despite having six acres to call her own, Daisy generally did not wander far from the house. Knowing this, we were immediately concerned when we came home one evening and she did not greet us with her food begging howl. Our primary search of all her likely hangouts turned up nothing. However, a secondary search found her doing the doggie paddle in our in-ground hot tub. We can only speculate that, either she wanted to relieve some of her daily stress by taking a therapeutic dip, or she simply got too close to the edge and fell in. Either way, she was now treading water and incapable of lifting herself out. She was obviously nearing exhaustion and barely keeping her nose above water. After being rescued by her human companions she ambled over to her closest resting spot and fell into a near coma state for the next 15 hours.

As the dog years passed, Daisy's "active" time was traded for progressively more sleep time. Additionally she was showing signs of physical and mental degradation. It may have been the cumulative effects of severe head trauma and near drowning experiences, or simply the results of aging. Either way she was very old, in pain, and as a result her temper often flared up without warning biting the hands that fed her.

We came to the conclusion that it was time to show her the way to the pearly doggie gates. The obvious course of action would have been to take her to the vet but we didn't want to cause her the additional stress and pain that would come during the process of transporting her. Not to mention, given her unpleasant temperament of late, we wanted to avoid losing any fingers while trying to corral her and lift her into a vehicle. While discussing our dilemma with a neighbor, who happened to be a nurse, she suggested that a couple of Oxycontin should do the trick. She also happened to have some that had been prescribed for an old back injury. In retrospect, this may have been wrong on several levels but at the time we were seeking the most humane solution and somehow drugging our dog seemed to be a brilliant idea.

On a sunny warm morning I solemnly said my goodbyes and ceremoniously fed Daisy a last meal consisting of narcotics wrapped in salami. Uncertain of the efficacy of the medication, I checked on her condition after the first hour and found her in a deep, relaxed slumber. After hours 2, 3, 4, and 5 she was still fogging the mirror. Hours 10, 11, and 12… no change. Somewhere around hour 13 she awoke appearing refreshed and with a new bounce in her step. She effortlessly (as much as a 16 year old dog dragging her belly and ears on the ground could) strutted around the yard stopping frequently to smell the roses, the other dogs' butts, and any other scent that her highly evolved sniffer and rejuvenated body could find.

Although Daisy had faced her share of adversity, throughout her life she had the will power to keep moving forward and not give up. Another 3.5

dog years passed before Daisy finally humanely and peacefully joined the big kennel in the sky.

The Lesson – Don't Give Up On Them

As leaders, we have all probably had our share of Daisys in our work force. Not necessarily people that have been hit in the head with golf balls, but people that have been cherished parts of our work family who have just lost their way. Too many times we give up on them and try to put them out of their misery, when they may still have some life in them.

Jack Welch, once considered one of the most charismatic leaders in modern business, had a controversial management practice called "differentiation", which clearly illustrates the point. Under the practice of differentiation, each business manager is required to assess their people and place them into three categories in terms of performance: top 20%; middle 70% and bottom 10%. The top 20% were treated like the stars that they were, and the bottom 10% were helped to find a new career inside or outside the company that better suited them.

The Daisy principle applies to the management of the middle 70%. The management challenge with that group lies in continuing to motivate the people in the top tier of the 70%, because the gap between them and the top 20% may be very thin. The bottom tier of the 70% is where the Daisys can be found, and it would be very easy for management to write them off and let them fall into the bottom 10% on the next go around.

It's the management of this middle group that has generated much of the controversy and disagreement with the concept of differentiation. But in Welch's words, "…the existence of a middle 70 forces companies to manage themselves better. It forces managers to scrutinize people more closely than they would ordinarily and to provide more consistent, candid feedback." Properly done, differentiation can help to energize the people close to the top 20% to work toward getting there, and through effective management, training and development keep those nearing the bottom 10%, from becoming Daisys who don't revive. Once again, quoting Mr. Welch, "Giving people self- confidence is by far the most important thing that I can do because then they will act." And getting people to act is what leadership is all about.

Chapter 5

Don't Be Cocky

The first non-traditional pets we obtained were chickens, and we have maintained a flock ever since. In keeping with our "don't eat our pets" policy we only harvest the eggs. Although our investment far outweighs the monetary value of the eggs, there is high level of gratification in feeding the family fresh eggs from free-ranging chickens. Not to mention that the chickens are the only pets we have had that have actually produced anything tangible of value.

At any given time we would have a dozen or more hens and a couple of roosters. Ordinarily they would play nicely with each other and with any other critters we had in the menagerie at the time. On the periodic occasions when things did not go well, it was typically the result of the chickens bearing the wrath of some ill-willed aggressor. Much to our dismay, over the years we witnessed various predators feast on our fowl including raccoons, weasels, and most disturbingly our own dogs. The latter, we quickly labeled as traitors, and after several misguided attempts to rehabilitate their natural instinct, we traded them in for more farm friendly breeds.

There were a couple of occasions, however, when our fine feathered friends turned the tables and became the aggressors. Of course, it was the roosters in the flock that attempted to show their dominance. This wasn't a significant problem until they tried to dominate their human caregivers. Such was the case with a pair of black polish roosters, which had the uncanny knack for detecting humans that would succumb to the ferocious fowls' intimidation efforts.

Performing daily farm chores took on an undesirable level of excitement for my wife Barbie who came to fear the frequent ambushes. Like sharks to blood, once the roosters sensed the least bit of apprehension in anyone, they would puff-up their chests, scratch at the ground as if to sharpen their talons, give a quick cock-eyed glance followed by a battle cry crow and then launch themselves with their razor sharp spurs extended toward their intended victim. Any exposed skin would be quickly decorated with bloody lacerations.

I personally experienced their attacks only a

couple of times. This may have been in part due to my consistent response which was a rather swift NFL style kick that resulted in a fairly impressive hang time and some immediate feather loss.

Barbie's approach was a bit more defensive. She would don knee high muck boots and bear arms. The weapon of choice may be a broom, a garden hoe, a hockey stick, or one of many other long handled utensils that one may find in your typical garage.

It became the norm for Barbie to dress for battle, and then cautiously commence with the farm duties, which would all too frequently climax with a barrage of Samari swings and earsplitting expletives levied by Barbie at the attacking rooster. Looking back I am embarrassed to admit that my reaction to this unsolicited aggression towards my wife was less than sympathetic. I was operating under the naive notion that we could somehow train these vicious creatures to become gentle birdies, or at the very least not draw blood at every encounter. Unfortunately, the more they sensed fear the more embolden they became.

The attacks continued until upon our twelfth wedding anniversary when I asked my lovely bride what she would like to do to celebrate our lasting love. Without hesitation, and with a tone that left no doubt to her conviction she replied "I want you to kill those damn roosters!"

Suggesting a clear violation of our "don't eat our pets" policy I answered "I'll kill them if you cook them."

With a devilish twinkle in her eye and an uncharacteristic venomous sneer she surprisingly replied "I would be delighted to…" Slightly frightened I gave a quick nod and headed toward the barn. I'm not positive, but as I retreated I thought I heard a high pitched cackle reminiscent of the OZ witch with the bad complexion.

In little more than the time it took to sharpen a machete and fire up the grill we were toasting to our anniversary over a meal of the toughest worst tasting chicken we had ever eaten… and we thoroughly enjoyed every bite.

Rooster encounter – episode II

I had just returned the day before from a business trip and we were all anxious to get some of the farm chores completed, so we could move on to other family activities. I was in the garage and had instructed my little girl, six years old at the time, to go outside and fill up a bucket of water. A few minutes later I heard some commotion and a slight whimper from over near the hose spigot. I ran out to find my daughter, Katarina, curled up in the fetal position with her arms up protecting her head. On her back between the two pieces of her cute little bathing suit were long red fresh scratches. As I tried to process what had happened I noticed our dominant rooster strutting back and forth about ten feet away. Barbie joined me as we inspected Katarina's injuries while consoling her.

After a brief debate with Barbie over the pros and cons of her intended use of the baseball bat she now clutched firmly in her hands, I was able to convince her to give Katarina a bath to thoroughly wash her wounds. With zero pre-meditation I proceeded to remove a handgun from the safe and shoot the rooster dead. The first shot accomplished my intended primary goal but the next five shots gave me some perverse gratification satisfying needs somewhere between paternal protective instinct and revenge.

Wanting to avoid attracting curious scavengers I promptly buried the lifeless bird in the woods on our property. Katarina, now into her dating years, is not entirely pleased when I look her potential suitors in the eye and honestly tell them, "The last cock that mistreated my daughter is buried in the backyard."

The Lesson – Know When to Pull the Trigger

Most people in the business world don't often find it necessary to shoot roosters who have attacked their kids. It's not unusual, however, to find it necessary to "shoot" something to which you have grown close, or to which a significant investment has been made. At times like these, in spite of how painful it may be, the best course of action is to just pull the trigger and not look back.

Once again, an excellent example of this comes from the space program, and a project called the "Checkout and Launch Control System," or CLCS.

For the entire Space Shuttle program, Kennedy Space Center prided itself on the fact that its Launch Processing System (LPS) had never been the cause of a launch delay. The system was developed at the beginning of the Space Shuttle program, and consisted of an array of custom built computers and operating systems from Modcomp, Corp. In the early 1980s Modcomp, Corp. began losing market share to companies like Digital Equipment Corp. and eventually dissolved its hardware and software businesses.

When that happened, Kennedy Space Center took on the hardware and software maintenance responsibilities themselves for the LPS, acquiring as many spare parts as they could from the defunct manufacturer. By the mid-1990s, however, the maintenance costs were growing significantly and spare parts were becoming more and more difficult to find. So in the mid-1990s, NASA began looking for alternatives. After an in-depth feasibility study, which included KSC NASA as well as contractor personnel, a decision was made to completely re-engineer the entire system, based on commercial-off-the-shelf components (COTS). The system was dubbed CLCS, and the objective was to assure the reliability, maintainability and performance for the remainder of the Shuttle program's life, with the least possible impact on NASA's taxpayer funded budget.

The project kicked off with great fanfare and optimism in 1997. The projected budget was $206 million and the schedule called for system completion to support its first launch in December 2000. It was also projected that, due to the COTS approach, it would be 50 percent less expensive than the 25-year-old LPS.

As the project progressed, the complete replacement approach began to be problematic. The development of over 3 million lines of software code proved to be monumental and adapting hardware to the task began to push the project behind schedule. By 2002, after several replans, and requests for additional funding, NASA headquarters in Washington called for a critical project review. This assessment concluded that, not only did the projected cost for completing the system escalate to $533 million with a completion date of 2005, the reviewers found that the resultant system could end up costing over $15 million more than maintaining the current LPS. The recommendation of the assessment team was to cancel the project.

Prior to making that recommendation, though, the team also reviewed maintenance plans for the LPS and concluded that with the annual reliability and maintenance checks, combined with regular modernization and safety improvements, the system was more than adequate to do the job for the anticipated years that the Shuttle would continue flying.

It was at that point that the political wrangling kicked in, because in addition to the $273 million that had already been expended, 110 NASA civil servant, and close to 500 contract employee jobs were at stake. But in the end NASA management evaluated the team's conclusions and agreed with the recommendation. A few days later, consistent with the stated willingness of NASA Administrator Sean O'Keefe and the Bush Administration to axe projects chronically over budget and behind schedule, workers were notified of the project cancellation. Even though virtually all of the NASA civil servants were reassigned, and the majority of the contract employees were subject to layoff, life went on at KSC. Through the end of the Shuttle program in 2011 the LPS was able to rightfully maintain their reputation of never being responsible for a launch delay.

Chapter 6

Ass Kickers

The primary duty of a guard animal is to discourage predators, usually of the canine type, from consuming your defenseless sheep. I naively thought that a Sheep Dog would be the obvious choice to guard our flock. This made sense to me for two reasons. First, Sam Sheepdog successfully worked in this capacity for the better part of the 1950's and 60's despite Ralph E. Wolf's (frequently mistaken for Wile E. Coyote) persistence and technological advantage through the use of various ACME products. Second, the most recent addition to our pack of dogs was in fact a Sheep Dog, which meant we could put him to work doing what I thought he was born to do. But apparently he was born to simply eat excessively large quantities of dog food, sleep twenty hours a day and bark at nothing during the other four hours, which typically were between 1:00AM and 5:00AM.

So, after consulting with local experts, we

decided we needed a donkey to take on the guard duties. A search of the local newspaper turned up the perfect candidate, possessing all the qualities that I knew to be important. That is to say, he had four legs, was a bargain price at $200, and had free delivery.

The jack (a male donkey or ass) soon joined our menagerie. My son Alex, fourteen at the time, like his parents had no passionate political party affiliation but quite cleverly gave our new arrival a first name of "Demo" and middle name of "Crat". As with any new arrival on the Ruehl farm, Demo (pronounced Deemo) received much pampering. With the exception of the pedicure given by the local farrier, he seemed to relish the attention.

Demo was good-natured and curious. He reminded me of an oversized puppy dog. He would follow us around the pasture and expertly sniff out any treats we may be toting. While on my knees mending a fence he would rest his head on my shoulder and give me a "whatchya doing?" look.

Despite his docile demeanor Demo took his centurion duties seriously. He was not fond of dogs or anything else he perceived as a threat to his flock of sheep. When aroused he would sound an alarm in the form a series of

Chapter 6

HEEEEEEHAAA's that were distinctly recogniza-
ble by everyone within a two mile radius. His
work ethic was impressive, often sounding off at
two, three, four o'clock in the morning, which
made him popular indeed with the neighbors.

His screeching battle cries were only half of his
arsenal. The more lethal component was the kicks.
Having hung around horses previously, we knew
enough to respect the rear end of any equine. What
I didn't expect was Demo's ability to kick lateral-
ly. I witnessed this seemingly unnatural talent
when Demo took offense to the farrier's pedicure
efforts and delivered a kung-fu style side kick. The
lightning fast kick extended perpendicular from
Demo's right hind-quarter and, fortunately, only
landed a grazing blow to the anticipatory furrier.

Life on the farm was relatively tranquil for several weeks until I received a tearful panicked
phone call from my wife indicating that her
favorite lamb, Chippawa, was badly injured. I hur-
ried down to our lower pasture to find Barbie
kneeling next to the white fleeced lamb which lay
motionless on its side. Sobbing she explained that
she suspected "that damn donkey" kicked her
beloved Chippawa. Sensitive to my wife's dis-
traught condition I spared both of us the pain of
any ill-timed mint jelly jokes. Instead I examined
the young sheep a bit closer. She was still breath-

ing but otherwise not moving. In the middle of her right side was a horseshoe shaped mark, leaving little doubt that Demo had in fact kicked a young member of the flock he was charged to protect. After a few minutes of gentle massaging and kind words I lifted the little lamb on to her feet. Much to my surprise she gave a quick BAAA and darted off to munch on some lush green grass.

With the diminishing likelihood of having fresh lamb for dinner my immediate attention turned to Demo. What possibly could be his motivation in doing harm to those that he so unselfishly protects? Barbie was far less concerned about establishing the "why" than she was about removing the threat. Sensing a limited window of opportunity to prevent further injuries and simultaneously save Demo's job, I promptly began questioning trusted neighbors who have more knowledge on such matters than I. The consensus was that Demo was protecting his food from the ravenous lambs. We had unwittingly set the stage for this to occur by feeding both the donkey and the sheep in the same pasture using feed bowls placed on the ground. Simple solutions included either feeding them in separate locations or raising Demo's feed station to a level that the sheep could not reach.

Unconvinced of this theory and unwilling to take the risk that the donkey may stomp one of the lambs into chops, Barbie promptly sold my Ass to the first person willing to pay.

The Lesson – Make the Right Hires

Many companies experience situations similar to the Demo crisis in their hiring process. Most managers have brought new resources on board with the greatest expectations, only to find out a short time later that it's not working out. In a 2009 Harvard Business Review article, Fernández-Aráoz, Groysberg, and Nohria explored some of the reasons this occurs and how to improve the probability of making a good hire. Their research focused primarily on hiring at the executive level, but many of the same guidelines are appropriate at all levels.

One of the biggest problems the HBR article points out is that most companies react to hiring situations as emergencies, hiring only when the need arises. Further, the actual hiring process in most companies tends to be relatively vague and inconsistent. For the most part companies rely on subjective personal preferences, gut feel of the hiring manager, and number of years of work experience rather than on such things as adaptability, teaming skills, ability to assimilate into the company culture, and a readiness to learn new things.

Failure to specifically define the critical success factors for the job being filled is another shortcoming.

Fernández-Aráoz, Groysberg, and Nohria propose a seven step process, starting with anticipating the need. This requires regularly scheduled and ongoing analysis of future needs. Focusing just on the current needs is insufficient for ensuring long term success. The next step is specifically developing the knowledge, skills and attitudes that the candidate must possess. This requires close coordination with Human Resources as well as a consensus of key decision-makers.

In a 2010 article in Inc., Magazine, Mark Clark, an associate professor at American University's Kosgod School of Business provides similar advice. Clark says, "think ahead. A new employee needs to be part of the long-term corporate strategy – and if you can visualize where you want to be in five years, or even by next quarter, it will be significantly more natural to see how a new employee fits into that matrix."

The remaining steps in the Fernández-Aráoz, Groysberg, and Nohria seven step process include developing the pool of candidates and properly assessing them against the developed criteria. The assessment process should be carried out by a small number of high-caliber, well-trained interviewers who have a stake in the result. It should also include detailed reference checks.

Once the appropriate candidate is selected, the deal should be closed as soon as possible, ensuring that the candidate fully understands the expectations for performance. After the employee is brought on board, they should be effectively integrated into the organization using a seasoned mentor. The final step is to audit and review the decision within one year. This should include appropriately rewarding the effective interviewers, and removing bad hires, which still have the potential of occurring.

A process like this takes time and effort, but in any business a little pain early on can go a long way toward avoiding "ass-kicker" incidents down the road.

Chapter 7

What the Experts Say

As our sheep matured we were quickly approaching our first lambing season. We had acquired a ram, a mature male sheep, which appeared to be performing his manly duties. Although difficult to visually detect due to the thick wool coats, we suspected we had several ewes, mature female sheep, which had been receptive to the ram's amorous actions and were now carrying our second generation of ruminants.

Most in the flock were of the Cotswold variety, which sported curly white fleece and white faces. Sydney, however, was a Romney with long earth brown wool and a jet black face. She stood out in the crowd not only because of her unique appearance but also due to her amiable personality. She would follow us around the pasture occasionally pawing at our legs to let us know she wanted a scratch under her chin or handful of grain. She was by far my favorite in the flock, and was the first place my wife Barbie promised to look if she was suddenly missing any of her jewelry.

Once confirmed by the presence of swollen udders, I proudly announced to Mike, my neighbor and dependable resource for local mountain wisdom, that our sheep were pregnant. Without hesitation he replied in a defensive tone "I didn't do it." With that cleared up our conversation moved on to what problems we may encounter during the birthing. Mike indicated that usually things go pretty smooth but if it is very cold outside we should be careful that the newborn lambs don't freeze to the ground. I had a momentary frightening vision of Barbie finding a hooves-up lambsicle in the middle of the pasture and me with three hundred feet of extension cord and a hair dryer in a futile attempt to revive it.

As we counted down the five month sheep gestation period, all of the expectant mommies seemed happy and healthy, and we eagerly anticipated the arrival of multiple bundles of joy. As the expected date drew closer we got into the habit trekking down to the pasture and checking for lamb ice sculptures every morning at 5:00AM. Within a four day period, one by one, a healthy newborn lamb would appear until all the ewes had given birth except for Sydney. Another day passed and our hopes of another bouncing baby lamb

were replaced with concern as we noticed
Sydney's normally engaging personality switch to
one of lethargy.

When I explained the situation over the phone
to the local vet, he asked if I had performed an
internal exam. My initial thought was… Are you
serious?… I'm not inclined nor qualified to insert
my arm in the behind of a sheep. After a moment
of consideration, I realized that I know what a
lamb looks like therefore probably would know
one if I felt it in the dark, I know which end to
enter, and lastly I might be able to save the financial pain of a veterinarian house call. Besides, in a
former career I was an EMT, I thought to myself…
which actually has no applicability to the task at
hand other than not being squeamish around various body fluids. "I'll call you back shortly" I
replied to the vet.

Sydney seemed even less pleased than me
regarding the exam. As I maneuvered my hand
into position I instantly recognized the strong
stench of infection. After groping around for a few
seconds I found an appendage that felt like a
cracked walnut shell. I went over in my mind the
various parts of a lamb in an attempt to match one
up with what I was feeling. At this point, confused
and severely doubting my veterinarian skills, I
decided to call in the expert.

As our vet performed Sydney's second internal
exam for the day, he said "That doesn't feel right."
He then proceeded to pull out a nearly full term
dead lamb with a crushed skull. Now realizing
what I was previously palpating I asked the obvious question… "How would the lamb's skull get
crushed?!"

As he stuck his arm back in he answered
"Don't know" and then with some effort pulled
out a second lamb in the same condition. "You
may want to have a necropsy performed on them
to determine what the cause of death was" he
advised. The vet indicated that Sydney was very
sick due to the infection most likely caused by the
decaying lambs and said grimly "In vet school
they taught us the rule of four S's… Sick Sheep
Seldom Survive!" and in his expert opinion she
would not survive.

As he saw it there were three options. He could
euthanize her now, which would be the quickest,
easiest, and least expensive option. Secondly, he
could treat her, which would require him to visit
twice daily to conduct a uterine flush and adminis-
ter antibiotic and vitamin shots. Thirdly, we could
transport her to the University of Tennessee veterinarian school where she could receive care 24/7.

My initial reaction was to hook-up the trailer,
load up Sydney and begin the 3 hour trek to

Chapter 7

Knoxville. Fortunately, Barbie was far more
rational and posed the question to me, "Can you
treat her?" She went on to correctly point out that
in addition to the financial and timing hardships,
the stress of the trip may kill the already fragile
sheep. Obviously my affection, in a purely platon-
ic sense of course, for this particular sheep was
clouding my logic, so we decided to run with
Barbie's plan.

After a quick lesson from our vet, and instructions to call him if anything unusual happened, as
if pulling two fermented lambs with crushed skulls
out of a half dead wooly sheep wasn't unusual
enough, I was left with one vial of antibiotics, one
vial of vitamin B, one borrowed stainless steel
hand pump, and a shopping list which included
syringes, 14 gauge needles, and a bottle of surgical
scrub. At this point I was beginning to second
guess the decision for me to play vet, but never-
theless I dutifully managed to find all the items on
my medical supply shopping list and returned
home to set the alarm clock for 4:30AM.

The next day we awoke to a dark frigid mountain morning with the mercury at 18F. Now this
may not seem terribly cold for some, but for us ex-
Floridians we might as well have been in
Antarctica. As instructed, I filled up a bucket of
warm water and mixed in the surgical scrub to cre-

ate a tea colored brew. Barbie and I trekked down to the pasture with supplies in hand. By the time we reached Sydney our fingers were already numb from the cold which made managing the syringes for the injections especially tricky. Sydney was not terribly amenable to receiving the shots, and seemed to take some sadistic pleasure in the fact that during the process I clumsily injected small doses of her medication into multiple fingers on my left hand.

The next phase of her treatment involved the bucket of warm tea-like liquid, two sections of clear tubing and the hand-pump. While Barbie deftly held one end of the tubing in the bucket, worked the hand-pump, and pointed the flashlight beam at the posterior of the ill ewe, I maneuvered my hand and the other end of the tubing into Sydney's uterus. We continued to pump the fluid into her until the steady stream of tainted tea ran out of her and off my protruding elbow. As unpleasant as this task was for all involved, it did at least serve to warm up my right hand and lower arm enough to regain the feeling in my frozen fingers.

Miraculously, after repeating her "treatments" twice a day for two weeks, Sydney made a full recovery and returned to her normal playful self. Several months later our daughter entered Sydney in the sheep show at the state fair. As Katarina led Sydney around the judging ring the ewe's confident strut was evident. As if perfectly scripted for the ending of a children's storybook, Sydney's triumphant survival story was capped by winning top honors as Best in Breed. Sometimes the "experts" are wrong.

The Lesson – The Experts May Be Wrong

In every decision that we make in business, for that matter even in life, there is usually no shortage of "experts" wishing to advise us. Much of the advice we hear takes the form of, "It will never work" or "We've already tried that." In the worst of cases we might even hear something like, "I already know what the solution is" or "You don't know what you're talking about." And the fact of the matter is that anyone can be an "expert" in that regard for several reasons. First, most decisions, processes or solutions are never 100% perfect. So it's easy for someone to recall a relevant problem or failure, or experience negative or imperfect intuition. When that happens it's very easy to generalize the situation and "throw the baby out with the bathwater."

But the fact of the matter is that, whether heading an organization or leading a project, professionals must make decisions if they are to be effective, even if the decision departs from their area of expertise. In his excellent book, "The Go Point," Michael Useem, professor of management at Wharton School of business, provides valuable insight into the decision-making process, using decision templates.

Useem stops short of providing specific templates for different kinds of decisions, but instead provides the framework for decision-makers to develop templates most appropriate to the type of decision that needs to be made. At a minimum, though, Useem suggests that the template contain three main principles.

The first principle is to clarify the objectives involved, and then commit to making a decision, which Useem calls "Getting in the Game." When the objectives are unclear or the decision-maker fails to get in the game, the result is often no decision at all, and the outcome is determined by other people, such as the self-appointed "experts."

The second principle is what Useem calls, "consulting the inner circle." The inner circle is that small group of trusted individuals that the decision-maker considers to be loyal and reliable sounding boards, advisors and advice givers. It can't stop there, though, because the advice of the inner circle can sometimes impede the effectiveness of the decision. Since those in the inner circle usually think so much alike, there is always the danger of groupthink creeping in. That leads to the third principle; consulting the outer circle.

If the decision-maker is truly interested in looking at all sides of an issue, then consultation with those who have contrasting views can be just as valuable as consulting those who share the same view. This may not be easy for some, as a great degree of open-mindedness is required and egos can sometimes get in the way.

If a decision is particularly complex and/or in an area where the decision-maker has little or no expertise, that is the time that advice from a true expert should be sought, but care should be taken to ensure that the expert is credible and experienced, with a true background in the subject area. All experts are not created equal and some tend to cling to mistaken beliefs in spite of data that show otherwise. Sometimes too much weight is placed on recent events or multiple factors and weights are not taken into consideration. To put a statistics oriented spin on it, the assertion of any expert should be considered to be a hypothesis, and the decision-maker should seek to test it.

In the end, effective decisions are the responsibility of the person charged to make them, and all experts have limits. Research shows that nonexperts armed with an effective process or simple technology can often make decisions better than the experts.

Chapter 8

Runaway Ratites

After cycling through various guard animals to protect our growing flock of sheep we were again on the lookout for a protector. During a casual conversation with my neighbor Mike, a born and bred local whose practical knowledge I have relied upon as we flatlanders adjusted to mountain life, he happened to mention that Emus make excellent guard animals. As fate would have it, within a week I spotted an ad in the newspaper for a pair of Emus and could not resist the temptation to add these unique birds to our menagerie.

In case you're wondering, an Emu is an Aussie version of an Ostrich and a member of the ratite family which includes various large flightless birds. Full grown they are over six feet tall and weigh about 150 pounds. They have excellent eyesight and hearing, and can reach speeds of 35+ mph. Their extremely powerful legs are their main defense mechanism. They are naturally curious and generally friendly to humans. In short, they are everything you could ask for in a guard animal. And if by some chance they don't work out and you don't have some silly self-imposed rule about not eating your pets… they are delicious.

The owner of the Emus, Jennifer, graciously agreed to deliver them to us. I anxiously waited at the bottom of our property which butts up to the main road. This fenced in area contains a small pond, a lean-to and at the time, our flock of sheep. It is one of the few areas within our 20 acres that is relatively flat. Jennifer pulled onto our road and expertly backed up the horse trailer she was towing right to our cattle gate. Thirty seconds later with our gate and the trailer door open the two prehistoric looking ratites nonchalantly waltzed into their new home. With much amusement I watched them roam about exploring their new domain. In case you have never seen an Emu before, picture Big Bird after having a nose job and becoming champion on The Biggest Loser.

The pair seemed to be fitting in well striking the proper balance between being protective of the flock and friendly to the family. They also scored bonus points for making excellent conversation starters with neighbors and guests. With that in mind, I was not immediately concerned when a yet unacquainted neighbor from about a quarter mile down the road called me about two weeks after the Emus arrival.

"Are you the one that just got a pair of Emus?" the elderly country gentleman inquired.

With a detectable level of pride in my voice I replied "Yes, I am."

"Well, I thought you should know, they just ran by my house."

Pride instantly turning to stunned confusion I thanked the kindly fellow and hung up. I quickly realized that I had not given any thought on how I would ever catch a pair of 150 pound birds running 35 miles per hour down the street. I immediately called my neighbor Mike. The phone rang once and the familiar voice answered "You have to sneak up behind them and grab them by the neck." Now my head was really spinning. How did he know what I was calling about? How am I going to "sneak up" on these sensory gifted birds? What will happen when I grab one of these powerful giant fowl by the neck?

I tried to calm myself, "Ok, step one... go find them."

I donned my Aussie hat, hopped into our SUV and drove a little over a quarter of a mile down the road before I spotted who I assumed to be the gentleman caller. He pointed me further down the road as I slowly passed by gesturing a sincere

thank you to him. I soon came upon a gruff looking chap with a puzzled expression standing on the
side of the road looking through an open gate
towards a quaint stone house.

As I pulled alongside him and lowered my window, I uttered a question that would either lead to
finding my AWOL guard birds or an anonymous
call to the police regarding a possible escaped
psych patient. "Hello sir, have you seen two six
foot tall birds running down the street?"

"I think they are in my yard" the chap respond-
ed motioning towards the stone house. In his
speech and on his breath I detected good early
afternoon beer buzz. I also sensed that he was
struggling to determine whether the critters doing
laps around his house were a hallucination brought
on by consuming copious quantities of fermented
malts and hops or he was an unwitting participant
in some reality show involving exotic animals and
hidden cameras.

"What are those?" my newly acquainted neighbor asked with a complete absence of southern
drawl indicating to me he was not from these
parts.

Mustering up my best albeit poor country
accent I replied "Why them are North Carolina
chickens… we grow 'em big here."

Despite his slightly altered state and understandable confusion over the scene in front of him, he found the intended humor in my smart ass remark and chose not to shoot me or the enormous chickens for the time being.

As we deliberated over the situation it was obvious there were two challenges at hand. First, how do we capture the critters? Second, how do we transport them back home. For a brief moment I envisioned a solution involving a lasso and saddle, but realizing that my lack of lassoing experience was only dwarfed by my lack of Emu riding experience, I concluded Mike's advice to sneak up behind them and grab them by the neck was slightly more prudent at the moment. So, my thoughts turned to transportation. It was obvious that they would not fit in my Rodeo without messy alterations to the SUV or the birds (note to self... next vehicle must be equipped with a sun roof).

"You can use my van if you like" the temporary landlord of my runaway ratites graciously offered as he pointed to the right rear corner of his half acre lot. There heaped the remnants of what appeared to be a mini-van. As I drew closer I am fairly sure I could make out Lee Iacocca's hand print on what was left of the right front fender on this 1984 Dodge Caravan that surely was the first one to roll off the Chrysler assembly line.

"Does it run?" I asked, doing my best to be

respectful of his generous offer.

"So long as you don't try to go above second gear and give yourself plenty of stopping distance, you'll be fine" he replied.

The plan now taking shape, I had a momentary flashback of Dr. Peter Venkman exclaiming "I love this plan… I'm excited to be a part of it!" Realizing that Ghostbusters and my Emu taxi were produced in the same year gave me much needed added confidence.

In a Pavlovian effort, I vigorously shook the coffee can containing the feed I had brought along. Seeing I got the birds attention, I sprinkled some of the feed on the ground and sauntered away non-chalantly in an attempt convince my prey that I had absolutely no intention of choking them into submission. As I watched them stride over and gobble up the feed I circled back around behind them as stealthily as an Aboriginal hunter… well… in my own mind anyway.

Apparently the big bird duo were not as oblivious to my approach as I had hoped. When I got within five feet of them they swiftly took two graceful steps and tripled the distance between us.

This scene repeated several times. It was as if they had some super-bird sensory perception that predicted my every move. Discouraged but not defeated yet, I swore that if I was somehow suc-

Chapter 8

cessful in capturing my runaways I would never ever use the term "bird brain" again.

I was running low on bait and patience…I needed a new approach. I decided to attempt to entice them into the rear corner of the yard where the fencing would serve to cutoff their means of egress. I scattered some of the remaining feed within a foot of the corner post and backed away. The pair again approached and greedily consumed their treat. As I moved in closer I focused on the one nearest to me and lunged with outstretched arms toward his neck. With the fencing drastically narrowing his exit my quarry hesitated for a second which was enough time for me to close the gap and grip both hands around his neck. My feathered friend instinctively ran effortlessly dragging his 180 pound attacker across the yard. My experience as a wrestler and martial artist had no apparent value under these circumstances and all I could think to do was to hold on tight.

After a continuous battle that seemed to last longer than the last two minutes of an NBA game, the not so gentle giant tired sufficiently for me to guide him into the opened side door of the Caravan. I stumbled back to the front of the yard sweat soaked, out of breath, jeans muddied, shirt torn, hat dangling, and abdomen lacerated hoping nobody witnessed me just getting my ass kicked by Big Bird.

"I wish I had my video camera… you looked like that crocodile hunter guy" my new drinking buddy exclaimed.

I was eventually able to similarly "persuade" the second of the pair into the auto artifact. An obvious indication that I had received a blow to the head during my Emu grappling event was made apparent that during the turtle like journey back to their home pasture when I verbally chastised the pair for their inconsiderate behavior and threatened them with potentially becoming the main course for Sunday dinner. As they debarked the Dodge Emubile back on their home turf they gave me a knowing glance as if to say "you silly man… that was fun… and we know about your 'don't eat your pets policy'."

The Lesson – Sometimes You Have to Grab a Problem By the Throat

Chasing errant emus is not part of most people's job description. Similarly, most of us don't chase satellites either. But as this story from the U.S. space program shows, sometimes astronauts do, and there is a lesson to be learned from it.

In 1990 NASA launched an Intesat-6 communications satellite into low earth orbit on a Titan rocket. While the launch was initially successful, an error occurred prior to orbit insertion leaving the satellite, worth hundreds of millions of dollars, in a useless low earth orbit.

After two years of negotiations and planning the Space Shuttle Endeavour was launched on a rescue and repair mission in 1992. The plan was simple. The Shuttle would be maneuvered into a position within reach of the Shuttle's 50 foot robot arm, then a custom made "capture bar", held by a spacewalking astronaut, would be used to haul the satellite into Endeavor's payload bay and equipped with a small booster rocket so that it could be jettisoned into orbit. However, after two grueling days and fourteen attempts, the capture bar was just not working as designed. In fact, on the last attempt the astronaut gave the satellite a slight unintended nudge with the capture bar, sending it into an uncontrolled wobble, due to the gravity-free environment.

The five astronauts on board, along with Houston's Mission Control began to brainstorm. Working overnight, they came up with a plan. Three of the astronauts would go outside the ship, one of them standing at the end of the robot arm, and two others in improvised stirrup-like devices attached to the sides of the payload bay. The Shuttle Commander would navigate the vehicle to within eight feet of the stranded satellite. Then at just the precise moment, the three astronauts would grab the satellite with their gloved hands.

The plan sounded risky, almost impossible, but the next day the three astronauts ventured outside into the vacuum of space. They configured the footholds that would keep them from becoming satellites themselves, and the Commander began negotiating the Shuttle just below the wobbling satellite. Then at 7:59 EDT on May 14, 1992, 230 miles above the Hawaiian Islands, the trio all reached out simultaneously and grabbed the errant satellite. They held it in their grip for an hour and twenty minutes, while a fourth astronaut manipulated the robot arm from inside the Shuttle so that the capture bar could be "hard-docked" to the satellite. After that it was a "relatively" easy task to pull it into the cargo bay so that the rocket booster could be attached, and the satellite redeployed.

Life is full of problems and sometimes they can be solved easily, sometimes it takes a little more effort, and sometimes they seem insurmountable. The lesson from the astronauts is, when that insurmountable feeling comes up, it's time to stop, think the situation through, and then grab the problem by the throat.

The $17M Pig

Perusing the local newspaper for free farm animals may not be considered a normal activity in most households, but in ours it provided more entertainment than reading the Sunday comics. So it was, on a "Black Friday" when most were out grappling for gifts, I was happily at home reading the classifieds when "Pet farm animals looking for a new home" caught my eye. As I called the number in the ad, I had visions of a homeless herd of assorted famished farm fauna wandering the streets desperately searching for a kind soul to offer them shelter and rations.

"Hello, I am calling regarding your ad about a home for some farm animals," I said when a female voice answered the phone.

There was a long pause that left me momentarily thinking I had possibly dialed the wrong number. "What do you plan to do with them?" she asked pointedly. I judged her to be middle-aged

and given the serious tone in her voice I chose not
to blurt out the first thing that came to my mind...
"Depends... are they good eat'n?" Instead I
explained that my family and I have an affinity to
animals and would consider taking in those that
may need a good home. What followed was a thirty minute interrogation, with a barrage of questions covering details on our family make-up,
occupations, income, real estate holdings, financial
obligations, religious preferences and sexual orien-
tation. To this day I am unsure why I played along
in the discussion, and can only attribute it to some
type of masochistic curiosity about this obvious
peculiar lady and her animals.

She concluded the conversation by stating that
it would be OK if we came to visit her and the
animals to see if we would make a good fit.
Mentally exhausted I agreed to allow her to continue the grilling in person.

A week later we took the 45 minute scenic
drive to Eccentric Elsa's mountain abode. As we
navigated numerous dirt roads and were surely
passing just out of view the remains of many
moonshine mini-manufacturing plants, a wave of
trepidation rolled in as I realized that Elsa knew
enough about us to satisfactorily fill a child adop-
tion dossier and I knew nothing about her other
than her address and the fact that she was going to

expel a variety of her beloved pets.

As we rounded the final bend we found our-
selves entering a mountain top compound containing a modest sized home painted with vibrant
hues, a pristine oversized barn, and an array of artfully decorated animal quarters. It was as if we
had passed through some magic portal and arrived
in the Land of Oz. The 360 degree breathtaking
mountain vistas left no doubt why this remote site
was chosen.

We piled out of our vehicle, mouths agape and
began to explore this wonderland in a trance like
state. It was a world obviously created by someone
with an obsession for animal caretaking and a pen-
chant for artistic detail. There were animals of sufficient variety to fill a small ark. Each species had
its own perfectly manicured habitat including custom built residences clearly crafted by a master
carpenter.

We strolled by the proud domains of chickens,
geese, ducks, miniature horses, goats, sheep, par-
rots, steer, donkeys, and a pig. All of the inhabitants seemed to call out like greetings in various
tongues "Welcome to our happy home!" All
appeared to be in excellent health and quite content in sharing their slice of pet paradise with each
other. I announced to the family that if I were ever
reincarnated as a farm animal this is where I

hoped to live.

Lost in our exploration, we were somewhat startled when approached by a petite, silver-streaked dark haired, mid-fifties lady. She was wearing worn jeans tucked into her muck boots and a tattered sweatshirt donned inside-out and backwards. I correctly surmised that she was eccentric Elsa. As we exchanged introductions I detected a distinct air of sadness in her demeanor. Although she politely introduced us to all of her animal companions, giving each of them copious kisses and affection along the way, it was evident that her sullen thoughts were far from this seclud-ed enclave. On occasion she would snap back into the present time and place long enough to pepper us with a series of invasive questions, before she would drift away to her distant sulky preoccupa-tion. By the end of our guided tour of this pet utopia we had come to agreement on which of her extended family members we would be allowed to adopt. Making the cut were six chickens, two goats, and a pig.

We arrived back a week later at the agreed time with a trailer in tow. The only things that had changed were the deepening distraction of Elsa and the added presence of a female farmhand by the name of Jill. With the aid of Jill we easily rounded up the goats and chickens, and after Elsa

gave each solemn and tearful hugs and kisses, we
loaded them on the trailer. At this point I couldn't
help but feel as though we were kidnapping her
children. My heart felt bad for this obviously dis-
traught lady and I was on the verge of canceling
our arrangement and heading down the mountain
with an empty trailer. But I thought that somehow
that may have been worse by delaying the
inevitable painful goodbye. Not to mention that we
had already been vetted and fully intended on providing them a good, albeit inferior to their current,
home.

It was time to load up the free ranging matri-
arch of this eclectic collection of critters... the
female potbellied pig named Bob. White with
black patches and a large pink snout, she was 150
pounds of attitude. Bob happily trotted alongside
Jill until they got to about 20 yards from the trailer
at which point they spotted Elsa sobbing hysteri-
cally. The jolly pig sensed there was trouble and
stopped in her tracks. Despite copious coaxing
from her best friend, Jill, and an emotional plea
from Elsa the belligerent boar would not budge.
Once Jill realized the futility of their current
approach she jogged off and promptly returned
with an armful of apples. She placed one on the
ground a few steps in front of Bob who sniffed the
air twice and cautiously closed the gap between

herself and the tasty treat. Once within reach the hungry hog picked up the whole apple in her mouth and devoured it in a flash. Jill then laid a trail of apples spaced every six or seven feet right up to the trailer ramp. The swine's appetite defeated her initial sense of forbearance until she reached the ramp. At that point there was no amount of gentle persuasion, apple baiting, or begging that was going to convince Bob to voluntarily walk up the ramp into the trailer.

My buddy Barry had tagged along partly to assist, but mostly to witness first hand this Disney like mountain enclave. After ten minutes of failed attempts to politely prod the pig into the trailer Barry and I exchanged glances and knew it was time for us to "help" Bob the rest of the way. We approached from the rear on each side and had her wrapped up in our arms before she could flee. At that moment I learned the true meaning of "squeal like a pig" as Bob let out a deafening prolonged high-pitched scream that undoubtedly had all inhabitants within five miles believing that someone was being murdered up at the "animal lady's place." Equally as impressive was the pure power of this pig. It was no small effort for Barry and me to wrestle Bob into the trailer, and after doing so I was thankful that we escaped any serious injury.

Apparently our manhandling of Elsa's favorite

pet was too much for her because she darted off with her face buried in her hands. After catching my breath I turned to Jill and told her that I really felt bad about how upset Elsa was. Jill asked "Do you know why she is getting rid of the animals?" I shook my head and she explained "She can't afford to keep them any longer because she lost $17M in the Bernard Madoff scandal."

Miss Piggy, formerly known as Bob, seemed to settle into her new surroundings just fine. We treated her as one of the dogs which meant she was free to roam the property during the day but slept in the garage at night. She had her own bowl and sleeping area similar to her four new canine companions. It was apparent from the beginning that Miss Piggy craved attention and companionship. She would sit for a treat and then happily role onto her side if she thought there was a chance to get her belly scratched. She spent her typical day lounging around and going on occasional excursions to visit the sheep or goats.

A couple of weeks after bringing Miss Piggy home I heard some commotion coming from the garage. Upon investigation I found Miss Piggy having a sexual encounter with a Playmate cooler that I had stored in the garage. I was not sure on whether I should go back inside so I wouldn't further interrupt the "moment" or I should attempt to rescue my cooler. I chose the latter and quickly realized that it was a mistake. Miss Piggy took great offense to my intervention and darted towards me nipping at my knee caps while emitting a snort-squeal combo that left no doubt she was pissed-off. For self -preservation I relented and gave the promiscuous pig back the object of her desire.

Next I did what any conscientious pet owner would do after being attacked by a passionate pig... I went to the internet. Apparently, female pigs go in heat about every three weeks or so at which time they are in a state of mind somewhere between horny and ornery for a few days. In fact, after a couple days of marathon sessions with her Playmate, Miss Piggy returned to her normal docile self. For future romps we replaced the red and white cooler with a five gallon paint bucket that my teenagers had artfully decorated with a large red heart and the words "Miss Piggy's Love Bucket."

Over the next year Miss Piggy's antics and infamy grew. From neighbors we heard of her frequent road trips. In one instance she turned away two uninvited pedestrians that were attempting walk up our driveway. The principal of our local elementary school even promised his students that he would publicly kiss Miss Piggy if they collectively scored high on a standardized test. Although he was no "Love Bucket" Miss Piggy didn't seem to mind the kiss.

At home Miss Piggy's activities seemed to becoming increasingly mischievous. She began shredding the blankets that we had laid down for her bedding in the garage. On one occasion we found an empty beer bottle carton right where we had left it near the garage steps. Problem was we didn't drink any of the beers. After an exhaustive search and a misguided interrogation of the kids we located the missing bottles wrapped up in Miss Piggy's shredded blankets. She had taken them one by one and hid them in her bedding. I suppose it is not that uncommon to have a beer with a pig-in-a-blanket.

The final straw though was when she began defecating in random locations in the garage. In order to avoid a larger mess it became a 6:30AM ritual for me to perform swine excrement removal before backing out the vehicles. I was willing to tolerate this inconvenience and figured it was a small price to pay for the hours of entertainment Miss Piggy provided. However, my paying job required a fair amount of travel and that meant that the rest of the family was left cleaning up pig poo in my absence. Unfortunately my wife and kids didn't share my assessment of Miss Piggy's entertainment value and staged a pig intervention. We sold Miss Piggy for $17 to a family who had a male pet pig and peace returned to the household.

The Lesson – Sometimes You Have to Trim the Pork

According to the "Free Online Dictionary," the definition of "Pork" is: "Government funds, appointments, or benefits dispensed or legislated by politicians to gain favor with their constituents." We've all seen it in one way or another, but sometimes it's just so well hidden that we don't even recognize it. Consider the story of the maintenance and refurbishment activities for the Space Shuttle.

While the Space Shuttles were flying, there were two types of maintenance required on a regular basis. The first type was normal turnaround maintenance between missions. The purpose of this work was to repair any damage or malfunctioning equipment that may have occurred during the mission. Additionally, configuration changes were made, which were required to support future missions. These might include the addition of special payload bay mechanisms to support the next payload, or the incorporation of test equipment to support certain projects or experiments.

The second type of maintenance was called

"Orbiter Major Modification Down Period", or OMDP, which like any aircraft was required after a certain number of flight hours. This would occur about every five or six missions for each of the Shuttle orbiters, and would take anywhere from six to ten months, and sometimes longer, to complete. Due to the complexity of the Orbiter vehicles, this maintenance was highly labor intensive and usually resulted in the replacement of a large number of parts or components. A part of the OMDP process was to upgrade Shuttle components with new technology. Two notable upgrades were the incorporation of glass cockpit technology and enhanced drag chute capabilities, but many more enhanced features were incorporated into the vehicles over the 30 year life of the program.

All of the Space Shuttles were built by a NASA contractor in Palmdale, California, and early in the Shuttle Program it was decided that the best place for OMDPs to be performed was at the plant where they were manufactured. The normal routine maintenance between flights, however, was performed at the launch and landing site at Kennedy Space Center, resulting in the growth of a highly competent team of technicians and engineers at that site.

After the construction of the last orbiter vehicle, Endeavour, in 1992 it started to become apparent to NASA management that maintaining work-forces in both locations was not only redundant, but highly costly. To make matters worse, sending an orbiter to Palmdale for OMDP required a multi-million dollar ferry flight on the back of a modified 747, and a return trip after the maintenance was completed. As the NASA budget started to come under closer and closer scrutiny, NASA management felt compelled to look for alternatives. An in-depth analysis was conducted, which showed that the annual cost to have maintenance performed in Palmdale versus KSC exceeded $30 million.

Based on that analysis, NASA made numerous attempts over the ensuing years to consolidate the maintenance work in Florida. But unfortunately, each time the pork would start to become visible. The California congressional delegation time after time would use its influence with the White House to block all attempts. They were lobbied, not only by representatives of the primary contractor performing the work, who would lose up to 1000 jobs, but also of hundreds of small local contractors who provided material, instrumentation and components needed to perform the maintenance. As the debate went on, the maintenance continued to be performed in Palmdale, and the $30 million bill kept getting paid.

Chapter 9

Finally in 2002, as NASA budget constraints continued to worsen, and support for the International Space Station was in jeopardy of running in the red, NASA Administrator Sean O'Keefe announced that all maintenance would be performed in Florida. It was a brave move on Mr. O'Keefe's part, and it wasn't without significant pressure and criticism, but he realized that sometimes you just have to trim the pork.

Sheep & Shuttles 🐑

Chapter 10

The Show

"We're going to do what with the sheep?" I asked my wife when she announced that we were taking our fledgling flock to the show. She went on to explain that our daughter and she were going to "show" the sheep at the Western North Carolina Fair. It would be fun and we could win prize money if the sheep did well. I was not going to fall for the promise of future earnings... again... and I had no idea what showing sheep involved which led to my immediate skepticism and barrage of logistical questions.

My lovely bride played along with my interrogation and at the conclusion I was thoroughly convinced of two things. First, there was no way this was going to profitable or "fun" and I wanted no involvement. Second, I would be fully involved.

Step #1 – Preparing the sheep – Since the sheep became part of our little farm the entire family was very hands-on with their upkeep. Like a new puppy the sheep were showered with attention. At least twice daily my wife, kids, or I would visit with the sheep. We would leisurely and caringly feed them, check their eyes and gums for proper color, tend to their hooves, remove briars from their wool, etc… Everyone including the sheep seemed to enjoy and appreciate the devotion. Preparing the sheep for the show therefore was a natural and enjoyable extension of the care we were already providing. Apparently the sheep would be judged on their overall condition, their cooperation when being handled by their owners, and since our sheep were going to be entered in the "wool" as opposed to the "meat" categories, it was especially important that the sheep's wool look and feel good.

The week before the show our pasture was converted to a sheep salon and the primping began. Beards, butts and legs were shaved, teeth were brushed, ears were tagged, wool was shampooed and conditioned and split ends were trimmed. After all the beautification effort sheep covers were donned to protect their new hairdos from the elements reminding me of scarf covered elderly ladies leaving their weekly appointment at the beauty parlor.

Step #2 – Transporting the sheep – My primary role in this adventure was to transport the sheep to the show and back. At the time, we had two SUVs and no trailer. Since the show was only an annual event, I had no desire to purchase a trailer, so we asked around and before long heard back from a cattle farming neighbor who graciously offered to let us borrow his livestock trailer. The day before the show I went to his ranch to pick up the trailer. As I drove up the dirt road I spotted a conglomeration of mismatched parts, assembled in such a way to resemble something that once might have been towed behind a vehicle for short distances for the purposes of carrying a couple of malnourished calves. I looked around hoping to find something a bit more roadworthy but soon realized that I had found the borrowed trailer. A few minutes later I had it hooked up to the back of the Durango and cautiously headed down the road to load up our flock.

The goal on day one was to transport the sheep to the fairgrounds and unload them into their stalls where they would be spending the next couple of days. The loading process took place on a Friday afternoon and went fairly smoothly. The sheep were accustomed to being handled and were coaxed into the "trailer" simply with a handful of grain. Within thirty minutes we had the sheep, feed, harnesses, two bales of hay, various grooming utensils, and water buckets piled into our caravan. I was tentative during the 30 mile I-26 trek to the fairgrounds fearing the real possibility that at any speed above 40 mph I would begin losing parts of the trailer, and any speed lower than 65mph would attract the unwanted attention of a State Trooper to my unregistered, unlicensed, less than road worthy appendage. Barbie followed behind closely playing a dual role as a support vehicle and lead blocker in case we started losing sheep. I continually kept an eye on my mirrors half expecting to see my escort vehicle swerving to avoid creating road kill of our flock as they escaped one-by-one from the deteriorating trailer. Amazingly, we arrived at the fairground intact and all accounted for.

As if they knew their lives were in danger the sheep seemed anxious to debark their dilapidated carriage and settle into to their temporary abodes. The 10x10 sectional metal stalls were filling up quickly as competing sheep owners dropped off their flocks. I quickly unhitched our borrowed trailer in the designated parking area. My sense of urgency was not associated with any pending appointment but rather an attempt to avoid any quizzical stares from fellow sheep owners. Despite my haste I could not dodge a few astonished glances in my direction that seemed to shout out "Did you actually transport live animals in that deathtrap?" I did my best to avoid any further eye contact until I had distanced myself from said deathtrap.

Step 3 – showing the sheep –The next morning we arrived back at the fairgrounds shortly after sun-up in order to prep for the day's events. The entire arena was buzzing with BAAAAAs as the hundreds of sheep seemed to be calling out and then responding to their long lost relatives. The sheep owners scurried about in a frenzy of activities centered around last minute sheep preening. Many of the sheep were secured to individual elevated portable metal platforms, allowing the groomer to have a more agreeable angle, and being trimmed with delicate precision and then doused with Tresemme products by their attentive owners. The scene looked as though an enormous collection of oversized Chia pets were being pruned for display by master gardeners. My wife studiously took it all in and quizzed several of the more experienced handlers. She would wander off for a while and then reappear with some valuable tidbit on how to make the sheep more attractive to the judges.

Day one of the show was for junior handlers so our 11 year old daughter was going to get the first chance to be in the show ring with our sheep. Despite the fact that most of our sheep outweighed her there was little doubt in my mind that she could handle them provided they did not freak out at the site of their competition.

The sheep are entered into categories based on their breed, gender, age, wool type and wool color. Each sheep must have a handler escort the contestant into the ring. The handler's job is to make sure the entrant does not get loose and go on a wild show stopping rampage. Additionally, the handler is charged with the positioning of the sheep; head up, legs shoulder width apart, and judge's view of sheep never obstructed by handler. At the junior level, apparently the judges are as much focused on the handler's ability to control her sheep as they are on the quality of the sheep itself. With that in mind there was a fair amount of parental nervousness and pride as Katarina led Cherokee, our young female Cotswold sheep, into the ring.

There were eight other contestants in this category and the handlers ranged in age from 8 to 18. The judge viewed the group, barked some unintelligible commands while motioning with her hands and slight head nods, and then inspected each animal by feeling wool, parting gums, lifting eyelids, and palpating the backbone and buttocks. I fully admit that I had no clue what the judge was looking for but it was obvious to me that our little farm girl and her pet sheep worked well together.

Chapter 10

Cherokee dutifully obeyed Katarina's gentle direc-
tions despite the fact that it was the first time in
the show ring for both of them. Their collaboration
earned them a 4th place ribbon, which according
to proper sheep show etiquette, was to be exhibit-
ed by inserting it 1/3 into the recipient's jean's
rear pocket leaving 2/3 dangling for display.

   With similar results the day pressed on with
Katarina showing six different sheep multiple
times in various categories. Each time, the sheep
cooperated fully with Katarina and there were no
signs of rebellion. We would routinely witness
some of the handlers struggle with their sheep. At
times an obstinate sheep would dig in like a stub-
born mule and not budge despite the best efforts of
the handler to persuade otherwise. Other times a
wooly ruminant would make a run for it darting
towards the distant sounds of peddling carnival
vendors and screaming patrons, its leash dragging
behind until an alert quick-footed bystander was
able to capture the critter. I looked for a common
thread among the hapless handlers and shifty
sheep but could find none. The stressed handlers
and sheep varied in age, weight, gender, and
breed. Nearing the end of the lengthy competition,
still puzzled by the phenomena, I finally asked one
of the veteran handlers, as yet another escapee ran
by us, "So why are certain people having trouble

controlling their sheep?" In a prolonged southern drawl he confidently answered "Cuz they aint spent no time with them…"

In subsequent years we consistently participated in two shows per year. We ultimately purchased our own trailer which was only slightly less embarrassing and moderately less hazardous than the one we borrowed for the first event. Our commitment to spending time with the sheep remained and as we became more experienced the number of top three finishes increased. Conversely, there always seemed to be handlers present that were struggling with their flock and as time passed I began to understand and appreciate the wisdom of that veteran handler that I had questioned in the first show. In fact, if you expect good results from your flock you must give them the time and attention they deserve.

The Lesson – Be Prepared for the Show

Regardless of the business that an organization is in, there's always a "Show." If the business is sales, then the show might be that big presentation that will win the piece of business you've been pursuing for an extended period of time. If you're in manufacturing, the show might be the introduction of a great new product that's hitting the market for the first time. Whatever the show represents in your business, however, the chances of success are greatly enhanced when the preparation work has been impeccable, and sufficient time has been spent with the key components (the sheep). In the Space Shuttle business, the "Show" is launch day.

The work of preparing for a launch can begin anywhere from six months to two years prior to the actual launch. While there are thousands of hardware related tasks that have to be completed prior to rolling a shuttle out to the launch pad, there is a people aspect of preparing for each shuttle launch that is crucial to launch safety and success; launch team simulations.

The launch team is made up of hundreds of talented engineers, managers, specialists and scientists, all of whom gather together on launch day in centralized locations to monitor their respective systems and areas of responsibility. Their role is not only to ensure that the steps in the countdown are flawlessly carried out, but also to respond to any abnormality or anomaly that might occur. Just like the Astronauts, who begin training for a mission years in advance, and practice the things they will need to do in space, so too does the launch team practice their countdown. This is facilitated by the use of a sophisticated simulation system that can mimic all of the idiosyncrasies of a launch vehicle on the pad during the countdown.

The simulation system is led and managed by a team of talented computer hardware and software engineers, who have the ability to create normal and abnormal launch countdown scenarios. Prior to any countdown, the actual launch team who will be present on launch day, will have run through dozens of scenarios (the sheep) over a period of months. They will monitor their systems, take the actions that are necessary in normal situations, and be forced to respond to abnormal situations, which the simulation team has set up. The scenarios for each practice session are kept secret by the simulation team, so that the launch team is required to respond on the spot, just as they are required to do during an actual countdown.

Through the use of these simulation scenarios, the launch team becomes engaged with one another, and highly responsive to any situation that could arise during a launch countdown. By the time launch day arrives, the launch team has "spent enough time with the sheep" so that it is unlikely they will be faced with anything they haven't seen before. In fact, while launch delays have occurred due to hardware or weather, in the history of the shuttle program a launch had never been delayed due to the inability of the launch

Chapter 10

team to respond to an anomaly.

Sheep & Shuttles 🐑

"Some people talk to animals. Not many listen though. That's the problem."
  A.A. Milne author of *Winnie-the-Pooh*

Teachable moments abound and only a small fraction of them occur in a formal learning environment. So the real question is, "Are we observant enough to recognize the less obvious opportunities to learn from the everyday events that happen around us?" Valuable lessons may be gleaned from events surrounding everything from Sheep to Shuttles.

We hope you enjoyed the following 10 lessons learned from Sheep & Shuttles:

1. **"Sheep" ishness – Don't be Sheepish about business planning.**
   Planning takes time and effort, but is a necessary part of any successful venture.

2. **Birds and Bird Dogs – Manage Conflict.**
   Conflict is going to occur in any environment. Good leaders know how to manage it.

3. **The Intimidator – Eliminate intimidators.**
   Remember W. Edward Deming's 8th point: "Drive out fear and create trust".

4. Pushing Up Daisy – Don't give up on them.
Give all employees an opportunity to succeed.
Don't give up on them too soon.

5. Don't Be Cocky – Know when to pull the trigger.
Some projects are not going to be successful.
Know when to cut your losses.

6. Ass Kickers – Make the right hires.
Hiring is an important part of every successful
business. Take the time to do it right.

**7. What the Experts Say – The experts may
be wrong.**
Use sound decision making techniques because
the experts are not always right.

8. Runaway Ratites – Grab a problem by the throat.
When a problem seems insurmountable think it
through, then grab it by the throat.

9. The $17M Pig – Trim the pork.
Eliminate waste. Successful businesses are lean
and mean.

10. The Show – Prepare for the show.
Do what it takes to prepare for the critical
events.